UN-MONKEY YOUR BUSY MIND

REDUCE STRESS AND ANXIETY

P. R. GALLANT

Etheria Publishing

CONTENTS

INTRODUCTION   1

1. ABOUT THE SOLUTION   7

2. TECHNIQUES FOR IMMEDIATE   13
   STRESS RELIEF

3. ACCESSING DESTRUCTIVE   21
   THOUGHTS

4. CBT Cognitive-Behavioral Therapy   27

5. MINDFULNESS MEDITATION   37

CONCLUSION   53

APPENDIX   55

SCIENTIFIC STUDIES ON   59
MINDFULNESS

MEDITATIONS   61

ADDITIONAL RESOURCES   67

INTRODUCTION

A whirlwind of thoughts races through your mind, stealing your peace. You'd love to pay attention, but you're too busy chasing those thoughts.

People with quieter minds could never imagine the noise that echoes inside your head. They'll advise, "Just turn it off" or "focus on something good."

I understand how difficult living with a racing mind is, having once suffered from one myself.

Despite your best efforts, taming your wild mind seems impossible. You may have stopped trying.

Don't give up hope. You can take command of your mind again.

I offer this book knowing that you can learn to tame your mind, manage stress and anxiety, and get relief, just as I have.

Imagine what your life could be like once your mind is under control.

Before revealing a solution to anxiety and stress caused by a racing mind, we must discuss a few things. I don't have a magic pill. The information presented in this book can help you manage your mind, but it's not instant and requires your faith and commitment.

When I speak about **faith**, I'm not asking you to believe what I say blindly. Verify what I have to say. Have **faith** that you can change.

Don't let your previous experiences or unfounded reasoning hold you back.

I authored this book to help you see your mind differently. It offers methods that will quiet a racing mind and provide relief from stress and anxiety.

PRESENCE & MINDFULNESS

Throughout this book, you'll find references to the terms' presence and mindfulness. It's necessary to understand how this book uses them because they are important aspects of the solution. Let's take a moment to clarify some terms.

We speak about presence as though we all have a certain amount of it, because we do. There's the 'presence' of being somewhere. Like when we attend classes, we are present for roll call.

That's not the 'presence' meant in this book. We use 'presence' here to describe the quality of our awareness. It's not as simple as just being here, such as showing up for class. It requires that we be in this moment, mentally. Our focus is on what's happening right **now**.

This book also uses 'mindful' differently. For example, if someone says, "please be mindful of my flowers." They're alerting you to avoid stepping on their roses. That usage of 'mindful' lacks the deeper awareness used in this book.

'Mindfulness', for our purposes, means being conscious of our internal and external experiences in terms of thoughts, emotions, and physical sensations.

Mindfulness and presence work together. The quality of our presence depends on how mindful we are during each moment of our lives. We can improve our presence by practicing mindfulness.

Mindfulness is not a far-away, magical state, but an everyday mental ability.

To quote a meditation master, "Even children, drunkards, madmen, and those without literacy, can practice mindfulness."

I hope you find these explanations helpful as you continue reading.

THE SECTIONS OF THIS BOOK

There are three main sections in this book, Quick Relief, CBT, and Mindfulness. Each section offers different remedies for intrusive thoughts and their resultant conditions. Below are brief descriptions of each section.

The Quick Relief Section goes through techniques to help you deal with intrusive thoughts, relieving the stress and anxiety that accompanies them. Methods in the Quick Relief Section are easy to do and calm your mind fast. Use these methods anywhere in almost any situation.

The CBT Section discusses how our thoughts, thought patterns, and mistaken beliefs cause the negative emotions we feel. Later in that section, there are exercises which allow you to investigate your thoughts and help you manage them for better outcomes and less anxiety.

To finish, the Mindfulness Section explains how awareness of thoughts and emotions can change how we experience life and bring us greater peace.

You may find one section more helpful than others, or that the combination of methods makes one brilliant solution for you.

Chapter 1

ABOUT THE SOLUTION

My wife and I operate a small wellness center in Brevard, FL, and we've met many people that battle anxiety and stress. They are my inspiration; you are my inspiration.

I've suffered these conditions myself. Most of the time, I was unaware of what was happening in my head. I lived in a state of agitation, confusion, and worry. I've spent decades learning what helps quiet the mind, sometimes a frustrating endeavor.

I've learned we must work **with** our mind to bring calm, and that thoughts and beliefs often get in our way.

We can't just do a brain scan to see where thoughts have carried us, or how beliefs developed over a lifetime make us miserable.

Methods in this book develop greater awareness. They help us find more helpful thought patterns and remove obstructions.

THE STUBBORN MIND

Have you noticed the more you fight with your mind, the more stubborn and unruly it becomes? It's like trying to fit into a dress that's much too small. You squeeze this part in, and others pop out. It's sneaky too! You think you have it quieted, then boom, another thought pops up. Like a sick game of whack a mole.

Your mind exists to protect you, *even at the expense of your sanity!* Therefore, you spend hours every day worrying about the future or regretting the past. It's your mind trying to keep you safe by reminding you how you've failed and warning you of impending doom.

Does your mind have the answer? If you could see all the thoughts happening inside that wild mind, you'd notice it doesn't. Many of your thoughts aren't even true.

GIGO

In computer science, GIGO means garbage in, garbage out. The same principle applies to our minds. When we are young, we develop beliefs to help us understand our experiences. These beliefs are just the best meaning our mind could assign. They aren't always truthful. Faced with stressful experiences, we access these mistaken beliefs; the consequences are rarely positive.

Our stress and anxiety can result from a single thought, triggering a mistaken belief, which activates more negative thoughts.

Round you go! Racing mind.

LOST IN THE FOREST

Lost in a forest, would you use a chainsaw to hack your way out? That's what you're doing when you battle thoughts to get peace from your busy mind. Attempting to shut down your thoughts will only frustrate you. Use your thoughts, like you would climb a tree in the forest, to get a better perspective.

Quieting your mind requires that you view thoughts differently. It's attachment to thoughts, a belief they're important, and identifying with them that keeps you stuck.

Let's drop the chainsaw and find a more effective way to manage your thinking.

THOUGHTS, PATTERNS, AND BELIEFS

Some scientists believe we have up to 6,000 thoughts per day. You can check my math, but that's about five thoughts a minute, or about one thought every twelve seconds. How productive can our thoughts be at that rate? Especially if you consider we sleep a third of the day.

We have so many thoughts we can't keep track of them, let alone stop them. However, we must become more aware of thoughts charged with emotion to avoid developing subconscious patterns that wreak havoc in our lives.

Over time, repeated thought patterns become beliefs. Often, these beliefs are about not being enough, not being smart enough, not good enough, not pretty enough, etc. When triggered, these beliefs can cause negative outcomes. Fortunately, we can change these beliefs that have become entrenched in our subconscious.

We'll discuss techniques to change mistaken beliefs later. For now, let's focus on quick relief methods that turn down your mind's volume and help get some needed peace.

Chapter 2

TECHNIQUES
FOR
IMMEDIATE
STRESS RELIEF

E arlier, we discussed presence and being mindful. There's something we didn't cover, how the quality of our presence affects our mental state. In situations where we feel stress or anxiety, it was likely triggered by negative thoughts which occurred because of our lack of presence.

If we increase our presence, we reduce intrusive thoughts and decrease our level of stress or anxiety. This is because there aren't any problems in the present. Our problems exist in thinking about the past or the future.

What problem do you have right now, at this moment?

Presence is important to your happiness because it allows you to fully experience your life, but it's also a great way to snap out of unhealthy thinking.

You can use the techniques in this section anytime that you're feeling overwhelmed with stress, anxiety, or racing thoughts. You might also use them in combination with others in the book. Mindfulness, CBT, and these quick help practices are all compatible.

When I'm feeling stressed, I don't always have time to pull up a cushion and start meditating or go through CBT exercises to understand a cognitive distortion. I use the following techniques.

Let's look at the first quick relief approach for stress reduction.

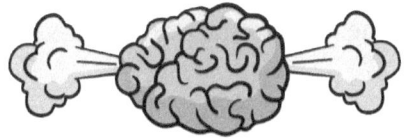

STOP

Many people are affected by stress. Left unchecked, it can lead to mental and physical illness. It's also a primary cause of conflict in relationships.

In moments of intense emotion, while lost in anger or panic, here's a reset switch, a stop button.

Example: You're studying for a test and notice you aren't absorbing the material anymore. Instead, you're lost in thoughts about how you'll fail and the potential impact on your GPA. This eats up your study time, adding to your feelings of anxiety. You need to stop these runaway thoughts.

Memorize the STOP method below. Use it when you feel overcome by thought or emotion.

Stop what you're doing, take a break.

Take a breath. Focus your awareness on your body as you breathe and come back to the present moment.

Observe: what is happening? Pay attention to your surroundings. Pay attention to ideas running through your mind. Don't become involved with the thoughts. If this becomes too difficult, return to just noticing your surroundings.

Proceed with whatever you were doing.

Use the STOP method for quick stress reduction. Notice how it gives you relief but also greater clarity about the thoughts and feelings you were having. As you practice this, you'll notice negative emotions when they first appear and can often find the thought that caused them.

RAIN

This technique allows you to explore your thoughts more deeply while providing relief from stressful moments. It's best used when you have a few minutes alone.

The exercise will give you a needed break from your negative feelings. It also gives your emotions the respect they need by allowing them rather than pushing them down or repressing them.

Example: Your friend says something that really pushes one of your buttons. You want to scream at her, instead, you muster the strength to excuse yourself and do this exercise.

Recognize what is happening.

Allow the experience to be there just as it is.

Investigate with interest and care.

Nourish with self-compassion.

RAIN is a terrific way to uncover those mistaken beliefs I mentioned earlier. During the investigation portion of this method, you're encouraged to look at your thoughts and emotions. Once you've used this technique a few times, you may notice thought patterns triggering your emotional reaction. These patterns could be the basis of your mistaken beliefs. We'll cover more about that in later sections.

BREATHE 5,4,3,2,1

Anxiety results from worrying about what's coming. We use the breath countdown intervention to reduce anxiety. The attention needed to perform the exercise challenges your mind. This brings you back to the present moment where you have no worries about the future, thus lowering anxiety.

Example:

You're sitting in a room full of people ready to compete for a new job. Your mind wastes time assessing whether you have an advantage over them. You fear you're outmatched and worry that your increased feelings of anxiety could affect your performance in the interview.

Sit in silence. Look around and notice.

· **5** things you can observe: your hands, the sky, a plant on the receptionist's desk.

· **4** things you can feel: your feet touching the floor, a ball in your hands, the pencil in your hand.

· **3** things you can hear: the wind blowing, children's laughter, your breath.

- **2** things you can smell: fresh-cut grass, coffee, soap.

- **1** thing you can taste: a mint, gum, the fresh air.

Did you notice how difficult it is to be lost in your mind while you're doing this exercise? That's how it works. You're taken out of your typical thought patterns and brought into the present.

Chapter 3

ACCESSING DESTRUCTIVE THOUGHTS

The exercises from the last section provide us with some reprieve. However, the techniques covered, while effective, are just band-aids. For long-lasting peace, we must observe the destructive thoughts that sometimes blaze through our heads.

BACKTRACKING TO THOUGHTS

If I suggested you focus your mind on the present moment and pay attention to your thoughts, you might want to choke me. Trying to keep still and just sit with your thoughts can feel like running to catch a speeding bullet train. By the time you finish this book, you'll become better at observing your thoughts. The good news is I'm not asking you to do that right now.

For this exercise, let's look at your thoughts from a different angle. Recall a recent situation where you felt a negative emotion (fear, anger, sadness, etc.), perhaps an argument with a friend or relative. Pick a moment that wasn't too difficult.

Try to remember the thoughts you were having.

Explain the situation. Who was there? What were you thinking? What emotions did you experience?

We'll use your answers later to further review your thoughts and beliefs.

For now, how does it feel capturing that pesky thought? Do you see how it caused your emotions and how thoughts around the emotion were also negative?

Great job finishing this exercise and discovering a new insight.

Insight: Our emotions are often driven by our thoughts, and negative thinking produces negative emotions.

A helpful mantra that I often repeat to myself while having negative thoughts is "What we focus on, we feel." No matter how long you practice emotional regulation, you'll have moments where you become lost in thought.

This mantra helps me to break the chain of unhelpful thoughts that might otherwise lead to negative emotions.

THOUGHTS AND FEELINGS

To gain control over our lives, it's essential that we take complete responsibility for our thoughts, emotions, and the resultant outcomes.

It's easy to believe we experience feelings because of someone else's actions. If that were true, it would mean that others handle our thoughts and feelings. Although a person may do something that causes you discomfort or pain, we decide how we respond to their behavior; we control what happens inside us.

While some struggle with this concept, it's essential to understand for personal growth and freedom.

Consider the following scenario.

Someone cuts you off while you are driving and having a bad day. You become angry and start screaming at them. He yells back at you in response. You Escalate the situation by pulling over and shoving the other driver. He takes it a step further and assaults you, resulting in you getting a fat lip.

On a different day, in a better mood, you would have brushed off the offensive driving and spared yourself the fat lip. Your response was your choice, not the other driver's. Since the same incident could occur, when you were in a better mood and have different results, you were in control of what happened.

You decide what thoughts to follow, what action you take, and the ultimate consequences you experience.

WHAT'S BLOCKING THE ROAD

We pick which thoughts to focus on and which thoughts to ignore. When our mind races, we're jumping aboard a thought train with no brakes, letting our mind decide where we go. One thought leads to the next: we become oblivious to our own mental activity and surroundings. It's like hearing a low-level humming sound. Our thoughts become faint, indistinguishable background noise. Imagine the possibility of bad outcomes when we're totally unaware of the ideas we're having.

So, here's the thing. We can decide not to follow that first thought, which leads us in circles. Remember, you have control, and you choose how your mind behaves.

Of course, you can't just force a peaceful mind. If we could, we'd all have one, wouldn't we?

Before we proceed, I think it's important to remember that we can't stop having thoughts. We'll always have ideas running through our minds. We can decide to abandon an unhelpful notion, but if you try to stop your mind from thinking, you'll just cause more resistance, stress, and more thought.

Chapter 4

CBT
Cognitive-
Behavioral
Therapy

We now know our thoughts have consequences and we manage them. Let's expand on this and explore how we can use (CBT) Cognitive-Behavioral Therapy to help manage our minds.

CBT has proven to be the most helpful way to regulate thoughts. It addresses mistaken thinking and focuses on specific outcomes. This means that you don't spend months on the couch talking about your childhood experiences. Instead, you analyze your thought patterns to find misguided beliefs.

A qualified CBT practitioner can usually help a person get over a mistaken belief and achieve their goal in three or four sessions.

USING CBT TO CURB STRESS & ANXIETY

We all have unwanted, intrusive thoughts. Mindful people can allow these to pass without reacting. Those with racing minds might never notice the thoughts and let them trigger strong, negative emotions.

While some disagree, stress and anxiety both have their roots in excessive negative thinking.

For example:

If you worry about the future, the repeated thought pattern will cause anxious feelings. Likewise, believing you will never make your deadline causes feelings of stress.

We don't need to argue, about which comes first, thought or anxiety. How about we just agree that we can manage thought? Regardless of when unwanted thoughts come, they are just that — unwanted.

CBT is the most successful treatment for stress and anxiety. It helps us replace unhelpful thinking with healthier thoughts. This can only work when we intercept a negative thought prior to acting upon it. If we react from our anxiety, rather than from a thought, our response would be automatic, and we couldn't change the outcome. There would be no remedy.

We use CBT to work with the following anxiety-producing thought patterns:

Polarized Thinking, or Black and White Thinking.

When our thinking is black and white (polarized), things are all bad or all good. There's no grey. This leads to unrealistic, negative conclusions. For example, though you won second place in a contest, you feel you lost.

Emotional Reasoning

A common CBT distortion, believing that feelings are fact. For example, you have a fear of spiders, so spiders are bad.

Personalization

A belief that other people's actions are because of you when they have nothing to do with you. In this type of thinking, you blame yourself for something that wasn't your fault.

For example, when you incorrectly assume your friends excluded you from something on purpose.

Overgeneralization

Believing that something "always" happens because it happened one time.

For instance, a friend asks you to do something for them and you feel like people always want you to do them a favor.

There are many more cognitive biases that affect us. Each of the distortions mentioned above has consequences. These can be minor, resulting in a short-term annoyance. Or they can be a long-term pattern that causes significant distress.

In all cases, thought is the trigger. Further, these thoughts cause negative emotions, which in turn cause undesirable consequences.

CBT EXERCISES

This section has basic CBT exercises that help you question the validity of negative thoughts and find alternatives. You'll learn how to reframe thoughts and reduce their negative impact.

Practice these techniques on yourself often for maximum benefit.

CBT QUESTIONING THOUGHT

Thoughts are always streaming through our minds. They move so fast that we don't have the chance to question them.

Our thoughts influence feelings and the way we act. It is vital we confront negative thinking. Take a moment to reflect on a negative thought you've been having.

Answer each of the following questions and write thoughtful replies. Provide detailed explanations for each response and explain why or why not.

THOUGHT QUESTIONING EXERCISE

What is the thought to be questioned?

1. What facts support your thought?

2. What facts disprove the thought?

3. Who's responsible for this thought?

4. Is this idea rooted in fact or feeling?

5. Is the idea black and white while the situation is more complex?

6. Is it possible that you are misunderstanding the evidence?

7. What assumptions might you be making?

8. Would other people have different thoughts about the idea?

9. Are you looking at all the proof or just that which supports your idea?

10. Is your thought the most likely outcome or the worst case?

This exercise helps us to view our thoughts from different perspectives. It also questions the validity of our thoughts.

What alternatives might there be to the negative thoughts you were having?

"WHAT IF?" TECHNIQUE FOR CATASTROPHIC THINKING

Catastrophic thinking is a very common distortion.

These examples illustrate catastrophic thinking and how we imagine the worst case will happen rather than expecting a more likely outcome.

- We might run late to work and think to ourselves, this is the second time this week I've been late, they're going to fire me.

- Your friend doesn't respond to your text fast enough and you think they must be mad at you.

Use the 'What If?' technique to reduce the anxiety that accompanies these thought patterns.

Ask yourself, What if? What's the absolute worst-case scenario?

Answering these questions can reduce your anxiety by showing you that even the worst-case result is usually manageable.

First, write your worry. Figure out the problem you're imagining by asking yourself, what are you afraid of?

Once you know what's on your mind, you can move on to consider how this concern will work out.

Consider the consequences if the catastrophe came true. What's the worst that could happen? Think back to see if something similar has happened before and how many times it has happened. Consider how often this disaster occurs and make an educated guess of the odds of the worst-case scenario.

Now Imagine what is probably going to come about—not the best possible result, not the worst possible result, but the most probable. Consider this situation and record your thoughts. How likely is this to occur?

Next, assess your chances of surviving this in one piece.

What are the chances you'll be ok in a week if your worries come true?

What is the probability that you will be all right in a month's time?

How about one year?

For all three timeframes, make a note of whether you would be all right.

Now, come back to the present and reflect on your emotions. Did the exercise help you relax, or are you still worried?

LET'S PUT YOUR THOUGHTS ON TRIAL

When we take time to scrutinize our thinking, we might find that our reasoning is poor. If we discover unhelpful thoughts, we can replace those with healthier ones.

The exercise below puts thoughts on trial. See if you can find alternatives to your negative thinking.

Begin by defending a negative thought that you have, and then build a case for why the thought is accurate, using only information that is factual.

Next, it's time to present evidence that disproves the negative thought.

Finally, take on the role of the judge, analyze the evidence, and form a conclusion based on reason.

For example:

1. The thought: My partner hates me.

2. An argument in defense of the thought: We sometimes argue about minor things.

3. An argument against the thought: we always resolve the problem.

4. The verdict: I'm upset when we argue, but overall, we have a good relationship. There's no evidence that my partner hates me.

Notice how the argument portion of the exercise removes the emotional charge by moderating the thought. See how the resultant verdict allows you to release the thought and abandon additional thinking on the subject.

These methods can make a significant difference in the quality of your thinking and reduce stress and anxiety.

Use these techniques as needed.

If you need additional help or wish to explore CBT further, you can attend workshops, or schedule private sessions. You'll find more information (Additional resources) at the end of the book.

Chapter 5

MINDFULNESS MEDITATION

M indfulness is about training your mind to be in the present moment. It gives us relief because the thoughts that disturb us are in the past or the future.

Meditation is the best way to work with your mind. To understand your mind and make friends with it, mindful meditation (mindfulness) is the way through the forest.

With mindfulness practice, we develop a deep awareness of our own inner workings. The thoughts that once carried us away become like clouds in the sky, just passing through. Negative emotion, once mindlessly triggered, ceases to hinder our best intentions.

When we aren't mindful, we're often so buried in thought, so unaware, that we don't even realize how little attention we're giving to what we're doing.

Let's illustrate with a short meditation.

See if you can observe what's happening around you without getting lost in thought.

- Set a timer for 3 minutes.

- Be silent for 3 minutes.

- Observe your surroundings. Notice the sounds, see trees outside the window, notice the sky, feel your feet on the floor.

A REVIEW OF THE EXERCISE

How present were you during the exercise? It's quite common for people to observe their surroundings successfully for a time and then become distracted.

What did you notice during the exercise?

Were you distracted by your thoughts or feelings?

What thoughts or emotions did you have?

The present moment is much fuller than our thoughts and feelings. Imagine what you miss when you're lost in the past or worried about the future. Many spend their entire life jumping from one thought to the next. When we're unaware, we might spiral down in sadness, anger, or guilt from thoughts we didn't realize we were having.

HOW DO YOU PRACTICE MINDFULNESS?

Mindfulness is about observing the mind. When your mind is busy, you watch the thoughts. As you learn to accept your thoughts without acting on them, they lose their power.

Example: You noticed that you had the thought, "I have an appointment at 3:00 that I can't forget." You can act on the thought and follow it to the next thought. "I hate the doctor's office." Which produces more thought, "What if he finds a problem," etc.

Alternatively, just notice the thought, let it pass by, then proceed with whatever you were doing.

This is how you break the chain of thoughts and avoid unnecessary stress! How important was that thought? Did you ask for it?

It will take practice and patience. Like training a horse, at first, your mind might buck and rear, but it will calm down, maybe even eat out of your hand.

I OBJECT!!!!!!

Please accept my attempt to address your potential concerns with as much openness and self-reflection as you can muster.

By now, you may have objections.

· I've tried mindfulness or meditation before, and it didn't work for me.

- I just don't have time for this.

- I've tried everything, and I'm tired of fighting.

- My mind is unique. You couldn't possibly understand.

Could your mistaken beliefs be deceiving you? You may never know unless you continue reading.

OBJECTIONS

I've tried this before.

How long did you give it to work? Were you patient, really committed?

Perhaps you could consider giving it another try. This time, be patient with yourself. Your mind has been running wild for a long time, and it will take effort to get it under control.

Solution:

Practice mindful meditation daily for 5-15 mins per session and at least 3- 5 times per week. You'll notice results after about two weeks or 8-10 sessions.

Another potential solution:

What type of meditation did you try?

There are many types of meditation. One may not work for you, other types might be just the ticket you need for your practice to thrive.

And another:

Where were you when you tried to meditate?

The best place to meditate is in a quiet area where outside distractions are at a minimum. Have you considered a qualified instructor or group that could support your efforts?

No time

A common excuse for not meditating is, "I don't have time." Perhaps the most curious because you can begin a mindfulness meditation practice with five minutes per day.

Nothing works for me. I've tried everything, but my mind is different. You don't understand.

Why resist positive change?

I'm sure that you want happiness, so why hesitate? Have I not explained the benefits? Are the scientific recommendations (see the back section of the book) inadequate? Are you closed to the possibility?

All I can say is YOU CAN! And when you are ready, I'll happily assist.

WHAT DOES A MINDFULNESS PRACTICE LOOK LIKE?

I hope you're starting to see the benefit of mindfulness practice. I encourage you to start a meditation journal along with your practice and write about your experience. This will serve several purposes.

· You'll be able to see your progress as you practice.

· In years to come, you can remember how your mind once raced and caused frustration. You can reflect on how meditation has changed your life and use it to fortify your continued practice.

Maybe even use your experience to write an instructional book of your own.

The Practice- Multiple Steps

The gap is an important goal in mindfulness, but first, you must increase your concentration.

That's an enormous challenge, right? Concentration is difficult when you have lots of intrusive thoughts, but it's the foundation on which your practice rests. I promise, it's not as difficult as it may seem. Remain patient and stay committed to your peace of mind.

MINDFULNESS PRACTICE STEP ONE

Develop Concentration

Do meditation for five minutes every day for the next two weeks. After those two weeks, give me 10-15 minutes daily for the rest of your life! Yes, as they say, this isn't a sprint, it's a marathon. While you don't really need to meditate every day, to be effective, you must meditate regularly.

I leave the details up to you.

Don't forget to write about your experiences in your journal.

MEDITATION INSTRUCTIONS

Exercises and Meditations (Also available in the Meditation Section, towards the end of the book)

Begin your practice with a concentration meditation. Five minutes per day, five days a week. Continue for three weeks. After that, increase the time you meditate by five minutes per day, each week, until you reach a half hour.

These are just suggestions. You can meditate for more or less than a half hour as it suits you. It's not recommended that you go over an hour as a beginning meditator.

CONCENTRATION MEDITATION

Concentration meditation uses the breath to focus attention on a single part of our experience. You continue returning to the focal point(breath) when you notice that you have drifted off.

This helps to develop concentration.

· Find a comfortable place to sit where you won't be disturbed.

· Close your eyes.

· Bring your awareness to your breath.

· Feel the sensation of the breath as it enters and exits through your nose.

· Notice the length, temperature, and depth of the in and out breaths.

· When your mind wanders off, gently return your focus to the breath.

If you notice that your mind wandered off, don't get frustrated, just continue bringing your awareness back to the breath. When you noticed that your mind wandered off, you were being mindful! The more you practice, the more mindful you'll become.

Each meditation has a specific purpose, some develop focus, while others increase presence.

If you join a mindfulness program, you will experience the different meditations in their proper order.

Note: It won't hurt to do them out of order. However, some meditations work best with certain foundations in place.

MINDFULNESS PRACTICE STEP TWO

Practice Awareness

Body awareness exercises are extremely helpful for those with stress and anxiety. The body is our best link to the present moment because the body and its sensations only exist in the now.

The body scan meditation is a fundamental mindfulness practice.

BODY SCAN MEDITATION

The body scan meditation uses the body as a focal point. We begin by bringing our attention to sensations in our feet and moving up through the body to our head.

· Find a comfortable position to sit or lay for this meditation

· Close your eyes

· Bring your attention to the toes on your left foot

· Notice any sensations you feel, tingling, heat, tension, or pain.

· Bring awareness to any tension or pain without trying to change anything.

· After a few moments, move your focus to your entire foot.

· Again, notice any tingling, heat, tension, or pain.

· Continue moving your attention up your body, feeling the sensations. Alternating from the left to the right parts of the body, right foot, left foot, etc. as you move your awareness up to your head. Noticing any sensations along the way.

BODY MOVEMENT

A great way to increase your body mindfulness is through mindful movements, such as YOGA, TAI CHI, or QI GONG.

It's difficult to be lost in thought while you're twisting your body into a pretzel. I'm kidding, but the sentiment is genuine. The focus needed in body movement will make you present, at least for a while.

Perform a body awareness meditation twice per week.

MINDFULNESS PRACTICE: THE GAP

*Didn't you say something about a **gap**?* Yes, I mentioned it at the beginning of this section.

"The gap is an important goal in mindfulness."

Then I hurried to concentration. That wasn't an oversight; we must first develop concentration and awareness before we'll notice the gap.

The gap is the GOLD. It's your FREEDOM.

Would you like me to tell you what the gap is already?

It's the quiet second or two between thoughts and actions. The action could be an emotion, physical movement, or another thought.

Do you sense freedom here?

When you develop mindfulness, you will eventually notice the gap. **It allows you to decide** rather than habitually following thoughts and destructive patterns of behavior. It also helps you avoid becoming lost in the past, or dreaming about the future.

You decide your focus.

Eureka, Gold!

MINDFULNESS PRACTICE STEP THREE

Broaden Your Awareness-Now, this is living!

Once you have your mind under control, you can expand your focus, and broaden your field of awareness, without losing yourself in thought. While keeping concentration, you open your senses to include everything around you. The trick is to observe without getting lost in any aspect of the experience.

This is called open awareness. Believe it or not, many people live their lives in this state. You can too! Follow the instructions for meditation at the back of this book and practice regularly.

Remember, you CAN quiet your mind. Don't give up! Continued practice is how you succeed.

HOW TO GET STARTED

- Study mindfulness.

- Continue meditation practice.

- Join groups that support your goals-Meetup has many. (Search mindfulness)

- Practice mindfulness and use CBT to explore thoughts, feelings, and beliefs that get in your way.

Best wishes on your journey!

FOR MORE
INFORMATION
ABOUT CBT AND
MINDFULNESS
OR TO ATTEND
ONE OF OUR
WORKSHOPS
VISIT THE LINK
BELOW

https://EtheriaWellness.com/workshops/

Conclusion, Exercises, and Resources on the following pages

CONCLUSION

L ike being lost in the forest. Once you climb a tree and get perspective, you will know where to go. If you see your thoughts for what they are, you will feel peace, clarity and release yourself from a life of distraction.

I hope you found this book helpful and achieve the happiness that comes with a quieter mind!

There are many great resources on mindfulness, its effectiveness, and how to practice. You can find some resources in the pages that follow.

If you enjoyed this book, please consider leaving a positive review on Amazon.

APPENDIX

Here's What Expert Practitioners Have to Say About Mindfulness

•

"The little things? The little moments? They aren't little."–Jon Kabat-Zinn

"Many people are alive, but don't touch the miracle of being alive."–Thích Nhất Hạnh

"When we get too caught up in the world's busyness, we lose connection with one another–and ourselves."–Jack Kornfield

"You are the sky. Everything else is just the weather."–Pema Chödrön

"Altogether, meditation is not to create states of ecstasy or absorption, but to experience being."–Chögyam Trungpa

"That's life: starting over, one breath at a time."–Sharon Salzberg

"Don't believe everything you think. Thoughts are just that–thoughts."–Allan Lokos

SCIENTIFIC STUDIES ON MINDFULNESS

National Center for Complementary and Integrative Health

"Many studies have investigated meditation for different conditions, and there's evidence that it may reduce blood pressure and symptoms of irritable bowel syndrome and flare-ups in people who have had ulcerative colitis. It may ease symptoms of anxiety and depression and may help people with insomnia."

Effects of Mindfulness-Based Stress Reduction (MBSR) on Emotion Regulation in Social Anxiety Disorder

Mindfulness-based stress reduction (MBSR) is an established program shown to reduce symptoms of stress, anxiety, and depression. We believe MBSR alters emotional responses by modifying cognitive–affective processes.

Mindfulness-based treatments for posttraumatic stress disorder: a review of the treatment literature and neurobiological evidence

Mindfulness-based treatments for posttraumatic stress disorder (PTSD) have emerged as promising adjunctive or alternative intervention approaches. A scoping review of the literature on PTSD treatment studies, including approaches such as mindfulness-based stress reduction, mindfulness-based cognitive therapy, and meta-mindfulness, reveals low attrition with medium to large effect sizes.

https://www.ncbi.nlm.nih.gov/pmc/articles/PMC5747539/

MEDITATIONS

CONCENTRATION MEDITATION

The concentration meditation uses the breath to focus attention on a single part of our experience. You continue returning to the focal point(breath) when you notice that you have drifted off.

This helps to develop concentration.

· Find a comfortable place to sit where you won't be disturbed.

· Close your eyes.

· Bring your awareness to your breath.

· Feel the sensation of the breath as it enters and exits through your nose.

· Notice the length, temperature, etc. of the in and out breaths.

· When your mind wanders off, gently return your focus to the breath.

If you notice that your mind wandered off, don't get frustrated. Just continue bringing your awareness back to the breath. When you noticed that your mind wandered off, you were being mindful! The more you practice, the more mindful you'll become.

BODY SCAN MEDITATION

The body scan meditation uses the body as a focal point. We begin by bringing our attention to sensations in our feet and moving up through the body to our head.

· Find a comfortable position to sit or lay for this meditation

· Close your eyes

· Bring your attention to the toes on your left foot

· Notice any sensations you feel, tingling, heat, tension, or pain.

· Bring awareness to any tension or pain without trying to change anything.

· After a few moments, move your focus to your entire foot.

· Again, notice any tingling, heat, tension, or pain.

· Continue moving your attention up your body, feeling the sensations. Alternating from the left to the right parts of the body, right foot, left foot, etc. as you move your awareness up to your head. Noticing any sensations along the way.

BODY AWARENESS

Use your body to bring yourself back to the present moment during your daily activities. The body is always in the present. Notice the sensation of your body contacting other surfaces when you change posture.

Example

When you sit down, notice the feeling of your body in the chair, your feet on the floor, etc. You can use a change in posture as a trigger to bring your awareness back to the present moment while standing, walking, lying, etc.

ADDITIONAL RESOURCES

MINDFULNESS MEDITATION

Meditation Groups

Search Mindfulness in an area near you. Meetup. https://meetup.com/

Workshops on mindfulness, Meditation, and Stress and Anxiety Reduction. Etheria Wellness. https://etheriawellness.com/workshops/

CBT

Beck, J. Beck A., Cognitive Behavior Therapy Third Edition. 2020. https://www.amazon.com/Cognitive-Behavior-Therapy-Third-Basics/dp/1462544193/

-Workshops, Breakthrough Sessions P.R Gallant. https://etheriawellness.com/workshops/

STRESS

Mcgonigal, K. Make Stress Your Friend. https://www.ted.com/talks/kelly_mcgonigal_how_to_make_stress_your_friend/comments/

Nccih Nih. Stress. https://www.nccih.nih.gov/health/stress/

Thank you for reading *Un-Monkey Your Busy Mind.*

THANK YOU FOR
TAKING THE TIME
TO READ MY
BOOK.

I TRULY HOPE THAT
YOU FOUND IT TO BE
A GREAT RESOURCE.
PLEASE CONSIDER
LEAVING A REVIEW
ON AMAZON.
-P. R. GALLANT

https://a.co/d/6Dzllqv

Conclusion, Exercises, and resources on the following pages

REFERENCES

Hanson, R. What Is Mindful Presence? Rick Hanson PHD. https://www.rickhanson.net/mindful-presence-2/

Murdock, J. (2020, July 15) Newsweek. Humans Have More than 6,000 Thoughts per Day, Psychologists Discover. https://www.newsweek.com/humans-6000-thoughts-every-day-1517963

Brach, T. RAIN: Recognize, Allow, Investigate, Nurture. Tara Brach https://www.tarabrach.com/rain/

Mayo Clinic Health System. 5, 4, 3, 2, 1: Countdown to make anxiety blast off. *https://www.mayoclinichealthsystem.org/hometown-health*

/speaking-of-health/5-4-3-2-1-countdown-to-make-anxiety -blast-off

Ackerman, C. (2017 Sep 29). Cognitive Distortions: 22 Examples & Worksheets (& PDF). https://positivepsychology.com/cognitive-distortions/

NIH. Meditation and Mindfulness: What You Need to Know. National Center for Complimentary and Integrated health.

https://www.nccih.nih.gov/health/meditation-and-min dfulness-what-you-need-to-know

Goldin P. and Gross J. (2010 Feb 10). Effects of Mindfulness-Based Stress Reduction (MBSR) on Emotion Regulation in Social Anxiety Disorder. National Library of Medicine. https://www.ncbi.nlm.nih.gov/pmc/articles/PMC4203 918/

Ramsay K. CBT Cognitive-Based Therapy. Achology. https://achology.com/the-academy-of-modern-applied-psychology/

Ackerman, C. (2018 Jul 10). Intrusive thoughts. Positive Psychology. https://positivepsychology.com/intrusive-thoughts/

www.ingramcontent.com/pod-product-compliance
Lightning Source LLC
Chambersburg PA
CBHW031251120626
46545CB00007B/2765